MICHIGAN'S CAPITAL CITIES

Written and Photographed
by

Melissa Stimson
M. F. Chatfield

MICHIGAN'S CAPITAL CITIES

Written and Photographed
by

Melissa Stimson
M. F. Chatfield

Thunder Bay Press

Published by Thunder Bay Press
Publisher: Sam Speigel
Designed and typset by Maureen MacLaughlin-Morris

ISBN: 1-882376-42-0

Printed in the United States of America

97 98 99 2000 1 2 3 4 5 6 7 8 9

We dedicate this book to our mothers.

TABLE OF CONTENTS

INTRODUCTION

We live in a unique state. The Native Americans, early pioneers and immigrants, inventors, and farmers—everyone who has survived the long, cold winters and has made Michigan their home—have made Michigan what it is today. In addition, the more than 13 million visitors that come here for their vacations have made tourism one of the state's leading industries.

Michigan also leads the nation in production of seven commercial crops and ranks fifth or higher in 25 other crops. This makes it the second most diverse agricultural state in the nation, with $37 billion in annual revenues. Michigan also grows the largest variety of trees in the United States, and products made from these trees add another one billion dollars to the economy each year. Ironically, Isle Royale National Park nurtures more than 30 types of orchids even though it is located on Lake Superior, the largest and the coldest of the Great Lakes.

Another dominant industry is automobile manufacturing. This flourishing business was born in Detroit and has made Michigan the Automotive Capital of the World. Michigan is also the nation's number one producer of salt and the Upper Peninsula has the largest commercial deposit of native copper in the world. More shipping tonnage passes through the Soo Locks in Sault Ste. Marie during the eight-month navigational season on the Great Lakes, than passes through the Panama Canal in its year-round season.

Michigan has 3,121 miles of shoreline, the second longest in the nation (Alaska is number one). It is the largest state east of the Mississippi and the tenth largest in the country. It is about the same distance from Ironwood in the Upper Peninsula to Detroit, as it is from Detroit to New York City. Michigan has more than 11,000 inland lakes and over 36,000 miles of streams. This means that no matter where you stand in the state, you are never more than 6 miles from water. It is truly a water wonderland.

Michigan has one of the longest toll-free interstates in the nation, I-94, which extends 275 miles from Port Huron to New Buffalo. With all of this natural beauty and significant access by water and land, no wonder Michigan was the first state to establish roadside picnic tables! Michigan was also the first state to guarantee a tax-paid high school education for every child.

We hope that this book itself will be a form of education by recognizing Michigan's capital cities and counties, the people and their heritage, the industries and their products, along with its productive farmland and rich natural beauty. We hope to create a strong appreciation for the grandeur of this magnificent place and what it has to offer its residents and its tourists.

The capital cities and counties are located throughout Michigan. The chapters are divided into southern lower Michigan, northern lower Michigan, and the Upper Peninsula. The dividing line between the 'south' and the 'north' is White Cloud in Newaygo County where it is said that "the North Begins and Pure Waters Flow."

SOUTHERN LOWER MICHIGAN

ALGONAC
Water Speed Capital
St. Claire County

Halfway between Detroit and Port Huron, lies the picturesque community of Algonac, the Water Speed Capital of the World, and the birthplace of the Chris-Craft Corporation. As early as 1817, this area shaped the shipbuilding future of the United States. Because of its prime location on the North Channel of the St. Clair River, which connects Lake St. Clair with Lake Huron, recreational boating has always been a great pleasure for tourists, summer residents, and locals alike. The multitude of islands surrounding the mainland offer extensive exploring for the landlubber.

French explorers journeyed to this area in the mid 1600s, mapped the new territory and prepared the way for the early pioneers. Fur trappers came in search of beaver pelts which were very sought after by wealthy French citizens. The first settlers of Algonac arrived in 1805, the year that Michigan became a territory of the United States. Samuel Ward started the Ward Shipbuilding Company in nearby Marine City, which became the largest of its day. In 1820, he built the *St. Clair*, the first lake boat to pass through the Erie Canal. Algonac became known as the home of boats built for speed. In the 1800s, that meant sailboats and steamboats. Both were produced in Algonac, and eventually the power boat as well.

Chris Smith, the postmaster of Algonac and a builder of duck boats, created the first powerboat. In 1894, he and his brother purchased a Naptha engine and attached it to a rowboat. Smith worked for two years to perfect his creation, which eventually achieved an astonishing speed of 9 miles per hour! Chris Smith was opening up the waterways of America by the turn-of-the-century, just as the Henry Ford was opening up the land with the automobile. By 1906, Smith had built a 26-foot boat capable of reaching a speed of 18 miles-per-hour. Smith teamed up with a friend, Baldy Ryan, and together they formed the very successful Smith-Ryan Boat Company.

In 1913, Ryan retired and the company became the C. C. Smith Boat and Engine Company—the principal owners being Chris, his four sons and one daughter. In 1914, they built the *Baby Reliance*, the first boat ever to reach a speed of 50 miles-per-hour. One year later, they built the famous *Miss Detroit* with the financing of a wealthy summer resident, Gar Wood. *Miss Detroit* won the Gold Cup, bringing it to the midwest for the first time.

Chris Smith and Gar Wood built boats in Algonac and raced together for the next six years. In 1921, they broke the official speed record at 80.56 miles-per-hour, which was unsurpassed for seven years. In the late 1920s, the Smiths decided to focus on the pleasure boating market. Chris's son,

Beautiful old boats can be found throughout the lakes and rivers of Michigan.

Hamilton, coined the name Chris-Craft and soon they became the world's largest producer of pleasure powerboats. Chris-Craft developed an excellent reputation for fine hand-built mahogany boats, which are now treasured by collectors and enthusiasts around the world. In the 1930s, it officially became the Chris-Craft Corporation and was based in Algonac with manufacturing plants in Ohio, Missouri, Tennessee, Florida, and Italy.

Gar Wood started his own company in Algonac and continued racing for many years. In 1932, he was the first to reach over 100 miles-per-hour in a race in Florida. That same year, his *Miss America IX* traveled 124 miles-per-hour in Algonac, making him a legend for many generations to come.

Several other boat yards opened along the St. Clair River during World Wars I and II and all of their contributions to the war effort were vitally important. Production of aircraft rescue ships, landing barges, and other naval craft took place in many of the local shipyards. Seaplanes were also designed and built in Algonac at this time.

Boat racing was very popular in Algonac (including ice-boat races during the winter) until the St. Lawrence Seaway was opened in the early 1960s, when the water became too rough because of the increased traffic. However, the boating legacy still remains a central theme in Algonac and can be enjoyed to its fullest during the summer months.

& For more information contact:

Greater Algonac Chamber of Commerce
P.O. Box 363
Algonac, MI 48001
(810) 794-5511

BRIGHTON
Snow-Making Capital
Livingston County

Brighton is the Snow-Making Capital of Michigan. It is located in the southeastern portion of the state in Livingston County, the fastest growing county in the region. Brighton was a stagecoach stop in the 1840s until the arrival of the railroad in 1871. Throughout Michigan's history, this community has continually kept up with the beat of changing times.

Mt. Brighton gives this area its title as the Snow-Making Capital. The resort opened during the 1960-61 ski season on a man-made mountain with 130 skiable acres. Of all Michigan's resorts, it usually opens first because of its expert snow-mak-

The "Snow Witch" is awaiting cooler temperatures.

ing abilities. The resort has over 160 snow guns; their largest pumps over 1,000 gallons of water per minute and can make one inch of snow in a one mile radius in one hour. Mt. Brighton has a patent on this powerful machine, called the "Schneehexe" which means "snow witch" in Austrian.

& For more information contact:

Mt. Brighton Ski Area
4141 Bauer Rd
Brighton, Michigan 48116
(810) 229-9581
or
Livingston County Visitor Bureau
(800) 686-8774

ALLEN
Antique Capital
Hillsdale County

Allen, the Antique Capital of Michigan, is located in the south-central portion of the state and was the first settlement of Hillsdale County. This county has over 350 lakes (15 over 100 acres in size) as well as the headwaters of five important rivers: the St. Joseph, the Kalamazoo, the Grand, the Raisin, and the St. Joseph of Maumee. With so much water, Hillsdale County offers outstanding canoeing, sailing, fishing, and swimming. Allen is situated on State Highway 12, formerly known as the "Sauk Trail," the main road between Chicago and Detroit in 1827.

In the 1840s, white settlers began to pour in, attracted by fertile farmlands and fast-growing, service-related businesses that catered to the many travelers that passed through the area. In 1843, the first railroad west of Toledo, Ohio reached Hillsdale, the county seat, making the town an important railroad stop. The rich industrial areas of Chicago and Detroit, coupled by local lumbering activity, attracted many affluent people to this area. These people brought fine trinkets and treasures with them, all of which were passed down through several generations.

As a result, Allen has become an antique buyer's paradise. Antique shops are located throughout the village and in the 1970s a group of local shop owners got together to discuss methods for advertising. They decided that the title of "Antique Capital" for the village would be a perfect way to

Collectibles are plentiful in Allen.

draw collectors to the area. Since 1974 they have held "Antique & Collectible Markets" with antique shops, malls, and flea markets on Memorial Day, the Fourth of July, and Labor Day weekends. The last weekend in September the village also hosts an Indian Relic Show.

& For more information call:

Hillsdale County Chamber of Commerce
3203 Beck Road
Hillsdale, MI 49242
(517) 439-4341

BATTLE CREEK
Cereal Capital
Calhoun County

Southwest of Lansing is Michigan's third largest city, Battle Creek, the Cereal Capital of the World. The city encompasses 44 square miles and is surrounded by gentle rolling hills and fertile valleys. The Battle Creek and Kalamazoo Rivers, along with many small lakes and streams, helped make the soil rich and fertile. It was perfect for the "Mound Builders," ancestors of the Potawatomi Indians, who once lived in this area.

In 1825, there was a small battle between two members of a surveying party and two Indians on the banks of one of the local creeks. Surveyors indicated on a map where the "battle by the creek" had occurred, and later the name was shortened to Battle Creek. The community was established in 1831 and was chartered as a city in 1859.

Battle Creek was an important stop along the Underground Railroad, the passage to freedom for many slaves. This 'railroad' was an informal network of houses, barns, and hiding places where slaves could get a meal and a safe place to sleep. They usually traveled at night, and typically their destination was Canada or a northern state.

The Battle Creek link of the Underground Railroad was guided by 15 civic and community leaders, one of which was Erastus Hussey, who held positions as state senator and mayor of Battle Creek. He helped found the Republican party and nominated Abraham Lincoln for president. Erastus and Sarah

Hussey ran a general store in front of their home. Together they helped more than 1,000 runaway slaves find safety in the 1840s and 1850s and literally put their own lives at risk by doing so. They aided Harriet Tubman, a very important figure in the underground railroad system. She and Erastus never met, even though Harriet led over 300 fellow slaves through the route 19 times.

Sojourner Truth was also born into slavery but eventually liberated. She made her home in Battle Creek for 27 years and was the first person to bring nationwide fame to the community. She was brilliant, speaking out for womens' rights and the abolition of slavery, although she could neither read or write. Both women are honored with many memorials and tributes throughout the city. Sojourner is buried in Battle Creek, while Harriet Tubman is buried in Auburn, New York, where she lived after the Civil War.

In 1854, an Adventist church was established in Battle Creek. The church grew quickly and the denominational name was changed to Seventh Day Adventist. Advocates of temperance and preventive medicine, they opened their first health retreat, the Western Health Reform Institute, in 1866. Ten years later, Dr. John Harvey Kellogg took charge of the Institute and changed the name to the Battle Creek Sanitarium. He expanded the basic medical treatment available and placed a special emphasis on fresh air, diet, and exercise. Lavish accommodations were provided for his patients. His brother, Will Keith (W. K.) Kellogg, became his business manager and together they made Battle Creek world famous. People came from thousands of miles away to seek a healthy way of life.

The Kellogg brothers invented cereal purely by accident. One day, while cooking wheat, they were called away from the kitchen. When they returned the wheat was stale, but they forced it through the rollers anyway to see what would happen. Each wheatberry was flattened into a small thin flake instead of a long sheet of dough. The flakes, when baked, were crisp and light and tasted wonderful. When eaten plain, without milk and sugar, the flakes were also found to be a dental abrasive and a gum massage agent.

W. K. Kellogg headed the Sanitas Nut Food Company, a mail order branch of the sanitarium for their former patients. W. K. saw the great potential and started the Kellogg Company. The company has manufacturing plants worldwide, but the headquarters are still in Battle Creek, along with several others. At one time, there were over 100 cereal companies based in Battle Creek, thus giving it the title of Cereal Capital of the World.

Cereal is considered to be a nutritional breakfast, but can also be the perfect snack, lunch, or dinner.

Post Cereal Company, started by Charles William Post in 1895, was one of W. K.'s biggest competitors. Charles was a patient at the sanitarium in 1891 and spent many hours observing the activities in the kitchen. Post had remarkable marketing capabilities and led the entire industry into success. The Post Cereal Company is now a division of Kraft General Foods.

During the Great Depression, the Battle Creek Sanitarium went into severe debt. High operating costs and a lack of wealthy patients eventually took its toll. In May of 1942, the U.S. Army bought the main buildings and the sanitarium moved a block north into the world's largest (until 1986) fieldstone building. The U.S. Army then reopened the former sanitarium as the Percy Jones Army Hospital until the fall of 1953. The building is now known as the Federal Center.

Since 1956, an annual Cereal Festival is held. The World's Longest Breakfast Table has become a tradition at the Festival, serving free breakfast to over 50,000 people. The Festival takes place during the first full weekend in June and begins with the Miss Cereal City Pageant. An Arts and Crafts show, 5K and 10K races, and amusement rides and games are some of the events included in the festival.

& For more information contact:

Greater Battle Creek/Calhoun County Visitor
and Convention Bureau
4 (River Walk) Center, Suite A
Battle Creek, MI 49017
(616) 962-4076

COLON
Magic Capital
St. Joseph County

There is no place on earth quite like Colon, the Magic Capital of the World. Located along the St. Joseph River, very near the Indiana border, this unique community is full of surprises. Colon lies between Palmer Lake and Sturgeon Lake in the far eastern part of St. Joseph County. Colon is a mixture of local townspeople and those of Amish heritage, combined with an influx of summer residents. But it's the magic, an ever-present reality, that truly makes this town unique.

This area was settled in 1831 and an interesting experience occurred regarding the selection of the name for the new settlement. After encountering difficulties in choosing a name, a local resident opened a dictionary and randomly pointed to a word. The word was 'colon,' which suited the spot exceptionally well as it lay between two lakes that are situated in the shape of the punctuation mark, the colon. The local residents agreed upon the name!

Due to the rich fertile land, farming naturally became a way of life. However, the summer of 1925 forever changed the course of history in this small rural community. Harry Blackstone, a prominent magician, visited Colon and decided it was a perfect place for his summer retreat from Chicago. He purchased an island on Sturgeon Lake that had all of the amenities that he needed: a main house, several cottages, and a barn. As Blackstone had a troupe with several employees and many animals it proved to be an ideal location to accommodate the entire crew, both for vacationing and rehearsing. Chicago was close by and it was relatively easy to transport the entire troupe by railroad to Colon.

After Blackstone met an old associate, Percy Abbott, at a magic convention in Ohio, he invited Abbott to Colon to go fishing. Abbott accepted, met a local girl and fell in love. In 1927, Abbott and Blackstone started the Blackstone Magic

Welcome to Colon!

Company in Colon which manufactured tricks of the magic trade. This business venture lasted only 18 months, dissolving because of a disagreement involving a magic trick. The two men never met privately or publicly again.

Abbott married and made Colon his home. In 1934, he opened a mail order business, the Abbott Magic Company. Ohioan Recil Bordener, an acquaintance of Abbott and a mind reader/magician, went to Colon to see him about improving his act. Abbott convinced young Bordener to become his partner and help pay for the mail order catalog. They remained partners until 1959 when Abbott retired.

The Abbott Magic Company held an open house for magicians in the fall of 1934 to demonstrate their newest tricks.

This was the first unofficial Magic Get Together. Magicians traveled from far and near to attend the event. In 1936, the local newspaper referred to the town as the Magic Capital of the World.

The annual Magic Get Together is now held during the first week in August. Wizards, ventriloquists, jugglers, and magicians alike—anyone who can fool the eye—attend the Get Together. From across the country and all over the world, people gather to watch the greats, such as Harry Blackstone, Jr., who was born and raised in the Colon area. For an entire week, spectators are stupefied by amateurs and professionals, while behind the scenes the performers share their secrets.

The Abbott Magic Company is now run by Greg Bordener (the son of Abbott's partner, Recil Bordener). The company is the largest manufacturer of magic tricks in the world. The

Blackstone and Baird rest in peace.

Magic Get Together is no longer held at the store because of the vast numbers of participants. The original magicians that attended the Get Togethers in the early years are often remembered. Although many are now no longer with us, their presence remains in Colon. Several are buried in the local Colon cemetery and the epitaphs on their tombstones reveal the personalities of a magical era. Even today the magic lives on and continues to mesmerize thousands of people who have discovered this magical place.

& For more information contact:

Colon Chamber of Commerce
P. O. Box 482
Colon, MI 49040
or
Abbott's Magic Company
(800) 92-MAGIC

KALAMAZOO
Bedding Plant Capital Kalamazoo County

Located approximately halfway between Chicago and Detroit in southwestern Michigan is Kalamazoo, the Bedding Plant Capital of the World. This city is also known for many other industries and four higher education institutions. It was originally named "Kikalamazoo" by the Potawatomi Indians, which means "boiling water," because of the whitewater rapids of the Kalamazoo River.

In the late 1700s, an European fur trading post was established. In 1827, the Potawatomi Indians deeded the land to the United States and it was surveyed by Titus Bronson in 1829. In 1831, the land was platted and called Bronson. However, Mr. Bronson was an eccentric man who alienated the first settlers. Within a few years, the settlers petitioned to have the village renamed Kalamazoo, a derivation of the original name.

A local land office was opened in 1834 and settlers arrived in big numbers including immigrants from Holland, Germany and Ireland. Because of its location between the two leading centers of the midwest, Chicago and Detroit, Kalamazoo developed excellent transportation facilities. Industries flourished and some of the early products were horse carts and buggies, paper, plows for farming, windmills, and cigars.

The Dutch inhabitants grew celery in the mucky riverbed land around the city and in the 1920s Kalamazoo became the

Celery Capital of the Nation. However, due to increasing competition from other areas, the celery industry declined and the Dutch farmers began to grow flowers instead. The plant industry began to thrive during the late 1950s. In the 1970s, Americans began spending more time in theme parks which use flowers by the truck load. People also began including flowers in their home landscaping, replacing them annually. The Kalamazoo Valley Plant Growers Cooperative was formed to regulate prices and marketing of the products, and has become the nation's largest with 60 grower members. Approximately 200 acres of Kalamazoo County's muck land is now covered with greenhouses.

Indoors and under the lights, bedding plants come to life.

Five million plants worth $35 million dollars were produced and sold in 1994, and even though Florida and California most probably surpass those figures, Kalamazoo is still known as the Bedding Plant Capital. New technology is providing an unlimited future for the local growers who, working in partnership with Michigan State University Extension Service, are leading the efforts in research and development.

An annual Flowerfest is held in the middle of July in downtown Bronson Park and throughout the county. Bedding plant displays, horticultural seminars, a flower show, and an art show are some of the wonders found at the festival.

& For more information contact:

Kalamazoo County Convention and Visitor's Bureau
128 N. Kalamazoo Mall
Kalamazoo, MI 49007
(800) 222-6363

LANSING
State Capitol
Ingham County

Lansing was named the state capitol in 1847. The Victorian-era capitol building became home to Michigan's government in 1879, and set a precedent for other states' legislative halls. The capitol building was renovated and restored in 1992 and offers free tours.

Nine fascinating museums depicting the many facets of Michigan's history can be enjoyed in Lansing. From the R. E. Olds Transportation Museum to the Telephone Pioneer Museum, there is something of interest for everyone. Throughout the four seasons, Greater Lansing hosts 50 days of festivals, including the East Lansing Art Festival in May and the Color Cruise and Island Festival in October.

Michigan State University's 2000-acre campus hosts Big Ten sports and an array of other events as well. Meanwhile, art galleries, music, dance and theater continually add a wealth of entertainment to Lansing and the surrounding areas.

& For information contact:

Greater Lansing Convention and Visitors Bureau
119 Pere Marquette
P.O. Box 15066
Lansing, MI 48901-5066
(800) 968-8474
or
(800) 648-6630

This Victorian-era structure influenced the design of other capitol buildings.

BERRIEN SPRINGS
Christmas Pickle Capital
Berrien County

Located in the southwest corner of the Lower Peninsula is Berrien Springs, the Christmas Pickle Capital of the World. Berrien Springs is right off U.S. 31 in the center of Berrien County, the heart of Michigan's cucumber country. The county consists of 576 square miles of low rolling hills (49 percent of which is farmland), 86 inland lakes and 42 miles of Lake Michigan shoreline.

Berrien County's earliest settlers were primarily of Norwegian and German descent. They became farmers or merchants because Chicago, and other nearby large midwest towns, made drygoods readily available. In the 1850s fine fabrics, crockery, groceries, ready-made hats and other clothing items could all be purchased. Strong and permanent communities were started.

However, the rich soil made farming the main occupation. Today, there are 12 farms in Berrien County that produce 280 acres of cucumbers for pickle processing. However, despite the fact that processing has been customary here, only one plant remains near Berrien Springs.

Now a blown glass version of America's most humorous vegetable in the shape of the Sweets and the Gurken pickle comes from Berrien Springs as well. In a Christmas Eve tradition which began in Laschau, Germany, a hand-blown pickle ornament was hidden in the boughs of the tree. The first child to find the ornament the next morning would receive an extra present from St. Nicholas or would get to open presents before the other children. People that grew up in the 1930s in southwestern Michigan remember pickle ornaments on their Christmas trees. With cucumber farms and pickle processing in the area, coupled with the German ancestry of the early settlers, it seemed natural for Berrien Springs to take on the tradition.

This tradition inspired a unique holiday festival that is enchanting a new generation of Midwesterners. The festival is held during the first two weekends of December and begins

This Christmas Pickle ornament will bring good tidings to the one who finds it first.

with a tree lighting ceremony. The Grand Dillmeister and a Christmas Pickle Prince and Princess are selected. A two-day Home Town Christmas Craft Show and a store window decorating contest sets the mood for Christmas. What better way to start off the holiday season?

There is also a community concert, Christmas stories read by Holly D. Pickle, and the Christmas Pickle Festival Parade complete with St. Nick, marching bands, camels, and reindeer, which attracts thousands of people annually, including Berrien Springs resident, Mohammed Ali. Many of the local merchants sell the blown-glass pickle ornaments, along with other popular items such as chocolate-covered pickles and clothing embellished with pickle decorations.

A truly remarkable sight in Berrien Springs is the 1839 Berrien County Courthouse Museum. The courthouse is Michigan's thirteenth oldest building and the courtroom is in its original condition. The Christmas decorations there are outstanding: the entire setting takes visitors back in time to the 19th century. Behind the courthouse, is the oldest standing example of a two-story log home in the state. It was built in the early 1830s for Berrien County's first lawyer. Some of the farms in the outlying area date back to 1855. This well-preserved community, with a relatively new capital title, has made its mark on the map as a place for genuine holiday fun.

& For more information contact:

Christmas Pickle Festival
Box 316
Berrien Springs, MI 49103
(616) 471-4031
or
Chamber of Commerce of Berrien Springs
1223 St. Joseph
Berrien Springs, MI 49104
(616) 471-9680

SOUTH HAVEN
Blueberry Capital
PAW PAW
Grape Capital
Van Buren County

Van Buren County has two capital cities: South Haven, the Blueberry Capital of the World, and Paw Paw, the Grape Capital of Michigan. Van Buren County is located in the southwestern Lower Peninsula along the shores of Lake Michigan, approximately 100 miles from Chicago. This county is in the western portion of Michigan's fruit belt and covers an area of 632 square miles.

The South Haven area raises more blueberries than anywhere else in the world. The town was first founded in 1833 but permanent settlers did not arrive until the 1850s. It grew rapidly and the lumber industry thrived there for more than 40 years. After all the virgin timber had been depleted, the land was put to use by farmers. Meanwhile, the resort business was well under way. It was started at the home of Mrs. H. M. Avery in the mid-1800s. Thousands of visitors arrived by steamer and train and by 1902 there were 215 resorts and hotels, several theaters, a casino, an opera house, and an amusement park with a roller coaster.

The first blueberry patch was planted in 1926 in the South Haven area by Stanley Johnston. He was determined that the plants would thrive there and spent a great deal of time and effort trying to convince local people of its potential success. He finally got support from his neighbor, Dr. Keefe, a dentist from Chicago. Together they located an ideal piece of property near Grand Junction alongside the railroad, just southeast of South Haven. They ordered 5,000 plants from a commercial propagator in New Jersey and the first Michigan blueberries were harvested in 1930. Stanley Johnston developed his own variety as well, the Bluehaven.

The fruit was packed and shipped from Grand Junction, sometimes as far east as New York or as far west as San Francisco. A blueberry growers association was formed in 1937, followed by an official experimental farm in 1938 where blueberries as large as a quarter have been grown. Today, the experimental farm and growers' association are in full swing in Grand Junction, with Michigan producing 60 percent of all the world's blueberries.

In 1963, the first National Blueberry Festival was held in South Haven to promote blueberries and tourism which had declined considerably compared to the early 1900s. The annual festival is held the second weekend in August and offers a variety of entertainment for everyone, including a youth pageant and the crowning of Little Miss Blueberry.

Southeast of South Haven is Paw Paw, the county seat and the Grape Capital of Michigan. Paw Paw is named after a tree found in this region and is situated in a very fertile valley. In the 1700s, the area was occupied by the Potawatomi Indians. The first settlers arrived in the 1820s and began to trade with the Indians. The location was attractive to settlers because it was midway between Detroit and Chicago and because the incredibly fertile soil was perfect for growing fruits and vegetables.

In 1821, the Potawatomi Indians signed a treaty in exchange for 50 square miles of land east of the St. Joseph River. In 1828, after increased pressure from the federal government, the tribe was reluctantly moved to a reservation in Kansas. Many protested this action and a ten year struggle began. In 1838, most of the remaining Indians were rounded up and escorted, by foot, to Kansas. A few of the more determined ones stayed behind to fight for their rights. In 1839, even these few were forced to join the rest of their tribe in Kansas.

The village of Paw Paw was founded in 1832 and quickly grew into a thriving farming community. Grapes were introduced in the 1920s and Paw Paw quickly became known as a premier growing area for this fruit. In the 1930s and 1940s, small wineries and juice factories appeared. Today the area produces 92 percent of Michigan's grapes and ranks fourth in the nation for grape production.

Grapes ready for harvest.

Each year, a Wine and Harvest Festival is held the weekend after Labor Day, attracting thousands of people from all over the Midwest.

& For more information contact:

Greater South Haven Area Chamber of Commerce
300 Broadway Avenue
South Haven, MI 49090
(616) 637-5171
or
Greater Paw Paw Chamber of Commerce
Box 105
Paw Paw, MI 49079-0105
(616) 657-5395

GRAND RAPIDS
Office Furniture Capital Kent County

Michigan's second largest city, Grand Rapids, has been known for over a century as the Furniture Capital of the World. This claim has shaped and molded the economy, culture and way of life in this southwestern Michigan town. Its supreme location along the banks of the Grand River, along with its close proximity to other major midwestern cities, has contributed to its great success as a center for the furniture industry.

The Hopewell Indians occupied this area from 300 B.C. to 300 A.D. They were followed by the Ottawa Indians, who settled in small villages along the banks of the Grand River. In 1787 this area became part of the United States. The land was purchased by a early settler, Louis Campau, for 72 beaver pelts and a trading post was established. White settlers began to arrive from New England. Many were skilled craftsmen of Polish, Lithuanian, and Dutch descent. Grand Rapids was on the edge of Michigan's great pine and hardwood forests, which provided excellent building materials for fine furniture, sparking the rapid growth of the furniture industry. By the turn-of-the-century, dozens of furniture factories flourished. They mass produced quality furniture at a reasonable price, making it affordable for the newcomers who were arriving in great numbers.

In the 1890s, the Sears Roebuck and Montgomery Ward mail order catalogs featured furniture made in Grand Rapids and boosted the industry to expectations higher than anyone had ever dreamed of before. The industry was also bolstered by a bi-annual "Market," an exposition of furniture and related products made in Grand Rapids. From 1878 to 1964, this Market drew vast numbers of people to the region which helped the hotels, restaurants, and area businesses to flourish as well.

Eames chairs from the 1950s.

During the Great Depression, production drastically declined. Many factories closed and those that remained worked together to redirect their focus. New ideas and designs using other materials were explored in the 1940s when metal furniture became the newest trend with the expansion of cities, skyscrapers, and government requirements for fireproof furniture in public buildings. Grand Rapids is now known as the Office Furniture Capital and continues to be a leader in the ever-changing industry of furniture building. From hand-made treasures to metal filing cabinets, Grand Rapids is clearly the forerunner. What will be next?

& For more information contact:

Grand Rapids/Kent County Convention
and Visitors Bureau
140 Monroe Center N.W., Suite 300
Grand Rapids, MI 49503-2832
(800) 678-9859

Also, be sure to visit the Van Andel Museum Center on Pearl and Front Streets in Grand Rapids, to view their on-going exhibit on the furniture industry (616) 456-3977.

CEDAR SPRINGS
Red Flannel Capital
Kent County

Twenty miles north of Grand Rapids, just east of U.S. 131, is Cedar Springs, the Red Flannel Capital of the World. Named for the bubbling springs in a grove of cedar trees on Cedar Creek this proud, middle class town of 3,000 people is dedicated to being a safe, quiet spot for working, living, and raising a family.

Long before white settlers moved to this area, the land was covered with a dense forest of huge pines and groves of towering hardwoods. Indian villages were located along the banks of Cedar Creek, which flows through the town. In 1851, settlers began to arrive and by 1863 the town boasted a population of 350. With the arrival of the railroad in 1867, Cedar Springs became the marketing center for all of the timber that came from Kent County as well as a trading hub for the vast territory that surrounded it. In 1897, 20,000 eggs, the largest shipment recorded for that era, carefully made its way to Cedar Springs.

In 1936, the entire nation suffered from an unusually severe winter. A New York newspaper published an editorial that stated, "Here we are in the midst of an old-fashioned winter and there are no red flannels in the U.S.A. to go with it." The two women who owned the local newspaper, the *Cedar Springs Clipper*, answered the editorial with a "red hot" rebuttal: "Just because Saks Fifth Avenue does not carry red flannels it doesn't follow that no one in the country does. Cedar

Springs' merchants have red flannels!" The story was picked up by the Associated Press and appeared in newspapers all across the nation. The original "Red Flannel," was a one-piece long underwear suit with a drop seat. Orders for the suit began to pour in from all over the United States. By 1939, the red flannel business was thriving and Cedar Springs became known as the Red Flannel Capital of the World.

Left: Red flannels decorate Cedar Springs year-round.

Right: Red flannels come in all shapes and sizes.

That same year, the town started a festival called "Red Flannel Day." It has been held annually since then and begins the last weekend in September. The entire town wears red on Red Flannel Day, the first Saturday in October, and anyone that is not better look out! In 1994, the factory was closed for a variety of reasons and it appeared that a tradition that had carried on for as long as some of Cedar Springs' residents could remember, was about to end. Two very determined women, Karen Williams and Cindy Davis, started their own red flannel company, KC's Original Red Flannels. With the help of 17 seamstresses working out of their homes in Cedar Springs, the Red Flannel Festival was held in 1995, with plenty of garments for sale. The red flannels are available by mail order and also at Cedar Sweets & Specialty Shoppe—the only place to get the original.

& For more information contact:

Cedar Springs Chamber of Commerce
66 S. Main, Box 415
Cedar Springs, MI 49319
(616) 696-3260

To order KC's Original Red Flannels
call (800) 763-3273

GRANT
Onion Capital
Newaygo County

The Onion Capital of Michigan is 25 miles north of Grand Rapids, via M-37, along the former Grand Rapids and Newaygo Railroad line. Farming has been the dominant activity in this quiet little town for decades. This rural community is situated on the edge of a fantastic recreational area 18 miles south of White Cloud where "the North begins and Pure Waters Flow."

Onions have a high nutritional value with heavy concentrates of vitamins A, C, and B6.

The history of Grant is similar to many other early Michigan communities. The great "iron horse" reached Grant in July of 1872 and opened up the area to the rest of the nation. Lumber and farm produce was shipped by rail to rapidly growing areas such as Chicago and many other midwestern cities.

Today, in Grant, one out of three people rely on farming (or related businesses) for their livelihoods. There are 14 working farms on approximately 1,500 acres, all growing onions. The most common variety grown is the Yellow Globe. The onion is said to be a cure-all with a heavy concentration of vitamins A, C, and B6.

Each year a Harvest Festival is held in honor of the onion. It takes place at the end of August, coinciding with the final onion harvest of the season. One of the highlights of this special event in Grant, even though it might make you cry, is the Onion Eating Contest!

& For more information contact:

Newaygo County Tourist Council
4684 S. Evergreen
Newaygo, MI 49337
(616) 652-9298

FREMONT
Baby Food Capital
Newaygo County

Northwest of Grand Rapids and 14 miles from Grant is Fremont, the Baby Food Capital of the World. It is the home of the Gerber Baby Food Company which was founded in 1928. Newaygo County has over 225 natural lakes and 356 miles of rivers and streams. It is one of Michigan's recreational havens, attracting thousands of people year after year.

In 1836, the region was inhabited by Indians, wild animals, and a few trappers. By 1837, the forests were razed by loggers who cut and slashed trees until the whole area was stripped of its virgin beauty. This, of course, opened the fertile soil for farming which quickly took hold. Vegetables of all kinds thrived and the county reaped huge rewards.

The Gerber Baby Food water tower is a symbol of a thriving farming community.

In the 1870s, the Gerber family, immigrants from Switzerland, settled in Fremont and established a very successful tannery. As farm produce was so abundant, the Gerber family started a canning company as well and in 1928, they began manufacturing baby foods. Fremont quickly became known as the Baby Food Capital. Today the company controls 70 percent of the baby food market, making it by far the largest in the world.

Each year in mid-July, the National Baby Food Festival is held in Fremont. It is one of the Midwest's biggest festivals and attracts approximately 150,000 people. This family-orientated celebration offers excitement for all ages, ranging from a Grand Parade, to the crowning of a Baby Food Queen, to a very serious Baby Food Cook-off. The Baby Crawl Race is always a crowd favorite. There is live music to entertain everyone, featuring nationally-known musicians such as country star Ken Mellons, alternative sounds from the Smashing Pumpkins, and old-timers like Three Dog Night. One of the most important members of the family is not forgotten either with the annual pet show. And throughout the festival there is a midway with carnival rides running continually. Every day, for almost a week, the activities are nonstop.

& For more information contact:

Festival Office at (800) 592-BABY
or
Fremont Chamber of Commerce
33 West Main
Fremont, MI 49412
(616) 924-0770

TRUFANT
Stump Fence Capital
Montcalm County

Just off the beaten track, hidden in a secluded valley, lays the village of Trufant, the Stump Fence Capital of the United States. One would almost have to be lost in order to discover this town. It is located in the eastern part of Montcalm County, 40 miles north of Grand Rapids and 8 miles east of U.S. 131. The county is comprised of 620 square acres and has over 200 inland lakes.

Fences such as this can be found on the outskirts of town.

In the beginning, the Potawatomi Indians hunted and lived in this area. By the 1820s white settlers discovered the virgin white pine groves and over the next 50 years, these trees, some 3 to 5 feet in diameter and towering 120 feet without a bend, were chopped down, drastically altering the landscape forever.

After the devastation of the forests, Danish farmers moved into the area. Frustrated by the thousands of immense white pine stumps left over from the logging, they dragged them with work horses to the edges of the fields where they found that the roots of the stumps intertwined with one another, making a strong fence.

One hundred fifty years later today numerous stump fences remain. Many of them are covered with vines and vegetation. Some have been saved and restored, others transported to new sites. A single stump can be worth as much as $500. Nearly every home in the town of Trufant has a stump or two in their front yard. Often you will see Jubilee Marigolds planted alongside the stumps, which is the Official Trufant Flower. The actual fences can be found in the countryside on the outskirts of Trufant.

Each year Trufant hosts a weekend long Jubilee on Labor Day weekend which hosts many activities, arts and crafts, and entertainments. A prince and princess and a queen are selected annually prior to the festivities. An old Danish specialty food, *aeble skiver*, is served each morning of the Jubilee. A cross between a pancake and a doughnut, it is made in a special cast iron pan that has seven deep indentations into which the sweet batter is poured and then fried. They are served with apple sauce, jam, or brown sugar.

& For more information contact:

Trufant Chamber of Commerce
P.O. Box 121
Trufant, MI 49347
(616) 984-2555

BETWEEN NORTH AND SOUTH

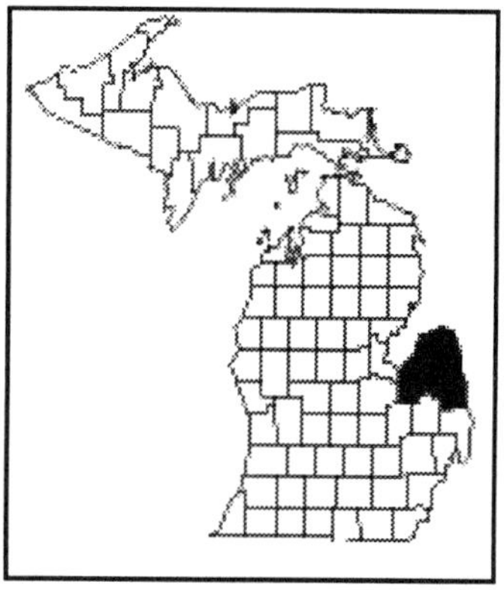

THE THUMB AREA

Bean Capital
Huron County
Tuscola County
Sanilac County

The "Thumb" of Michigan's Lower Peninsula, located on Lake Huron just north of Detroit, is the Bean Capital of the World. Huron, Tuscola, and Sanilac counties rank as one of the world's top producers of dry, edible beans. The majority of the beans harvested are Navy beans, one of the seven varieties grown in the state. Commercial production of dry beans in Michigan began over 100 years ago and products from this enormous industry are now sold throughout the world.

The thumb area is a product of the Ice Age when, about one million years ago, huge glaciers shifted back and forth. The now flat terrain was formed by glacial deposits and in the southern part of Tuscola County, some deposits are up to 250 feet in depth. As a result, the entire region is naturally fertile and not subject to erosion, making it ideal for farming.

Originally, the first people in the thumb area were hunters not farmers. They hunted beavers, elks, caribous and mastodons, a first cousin to the elephant. They are called Paleo-Indians by archeologists ('paleo' means ancient), as a way to distinguish them from other tribes that followed. Signs of Ottawa, Huron, and Potawotami Indians have also been found throughout this region, particularly near Saginaw Bay. Most of these bands of Indians were relatively small and traveled from one place to another. Petroglyphs have been found in

Greenleaf Township in Sanilac County, but their origins are a mystery; they could date back as far as 1,000 years.

When settlers first arrived in the thumb area, they found the Chippewa Indians living there. The Chippewa were hunters and fishermen, relying heavily on Lake Huron for fish as well as planting beans, corn, and squash. The settlers found virgin timber including white pines ranging from 125 to 170 feet tall with trunks 2 to 5 feet in diameter. In some places the forests were so thick that they completely blocked the sun. Fallen trees were piled as high as 8 feet tall and moss a foot deep was growing everywhere.

The thumb area was extremely difficult to reach and was often misinterpreted as an unprofitable growing region. Both factors slowed the development of the area. In the winter, before the forests were cleared, people traveled on the ice of Lake Huron and Saginaw Bay. Slowly growth began and from 1832 to 1881, lumbering dominated the region. Shingles were actually used in place of money! At a hotel, five meals could be purchased for 1,000 shingles; a barrel of flour for 10,000 shingles, and so on. At the northern tip of the thumb area, salt was refined and commercial fishing also became a popular occupation. The fish were salted and packed in barrels.

In September 1881, a huge forest fire wiped out nearly everything. Two hundred eighty two lives were lost; 15,000 people were left homeless; and 3,400 buildings were destroyed. When word of the disaster reached America's first chapter of the Red Cross in New York, relief operations were put into effect for the first time ever. Clara Barton, the first Red Cross president, sent supplies to the thumb area immediately.

Farming took over after the forests were cleared. The thumb area is now considered to be one of the richest farming regions in the world. Sugar beets thrive there, but beans are the mainstay. Sixty-five percent of the nation's Navy beans come from Michigan. The other major classes of beans grown are Cranberry Beans, Pinto Beans, Dark Red Kidney Beans,

Light Red Kidney Beans, Black Beans, and Great Northern Beans. The thumb area has a high water table, therefore the crops require very little irrigation. Along with superior growing conditions, Michigan has taken great measures to insure high quality beans. In 1938, the Michigan Bean Shippers' Association began a mandatory, point-of-origin dry bean inspection program. In addition, the Michigan Bean Commission was formed to increase productivity and quality through research and technology.

This bean elevator in Breckenridge, Michigan is an example of the industry's success.

Originally Saginaw was considered the Bean Capital because it was the trading center for the export of beans grown in the state. However, when the St. Lawrence Seaway was opened, export shifted to ports along Lake Huron.

The town of Pigeon in Huron County is home to the largest bean elevator in the world. Fairgrove in Tuscola County hosts the State Bean Festival every Labor Day Weekend, and just recently held their 50th annual festival.

& For more information contact:

Michigan Bean Commission
1031 South U.S. 27
St. Johns, Michigan, 48879
(517) 224-1361

NORTHERN LOWER MICHIGAN

MOUNT PLEASANT
Oil Capital
Isabella County

Located almost exactly in the center of the Lower Peninsula is Mount Pleasant, the Oil Capital of Michigan. It is the seat of Isabella County and the home to Central Michigan University. The area around this charming midwestern college town ranges from rolling hills to flat lands covered with forests and farmland. In the late 1920s, oil was discovered here and Mt. Pleasant became a center for Michigan's oil and gas exploration.

The first settlers arrived in 1854 and resided in harmony with the Chippewa Indians for many years. The Indians were exceptionally helpful to the new residents and they shared many celebrations together before the rapid development of the region. When the Civil War broke out, nearly 70 Indians from Isabella County enlisted.

But by 1890, the number of Indians had dwindled to less than half of its peak population and many of those who remained were living on a reservation. Those who did not were seen as impeding the growth of Mt. Pleasant by local businessmen because they were living on idle land that could be converted into productive farmland. The Department of the Interior was pressured to relocate these Indians. After some resistance they were "properly compensated" and forced to move on.

Farming was the main industry until 1928 when the Pure Oil Company drilled their first well and struck oil. By Sep-

day from 58 producing wells. By the end of 1930, while the entire nation was caught in the grip of the Great Depression, Mt. Pleasant was one of the few places to flourish. Other peaks in drilling occurred in the late 1940s, the early 1960s, and again in the 1980s. Several million dollars from the discovery of oil has been given to the state over the years to purchase land for state parks. More than 150 oil-related en-

Oil rigs such as this one can be found throughout Isabella County.

terprises are still based in Mt. Pleasant even though many fields are inactive. It is hopeful that new technology may boost production again.

& For more information contact:

Mt. Pleasant Area Chamber of Commerce
114 East Broadway
Mt. Pleasant, MI 48858
(517) 772-2396

HART & SHELBY
Asparagus Capital
Oceana County

Oceana County is the Asparagus Capital of the World. Michigan ranks third in asparagus production in the United States, just behind California and Washington. However, Oceana County grows the most asparagus per acre than anywhere else in the world. It is located exactly 220 miles from Chicago, Detroit, and the Straits of Mackinac, with its western boundary along Lake Michigan. The county is 536 square miles in size, has 65 inland lakes, and 48,000 acres of national forest.

The first white settlers came to the region in 1848 and established a sawmill at Whiskey Creek. In 1864, the town of Hart became the county seat. Nine years later, residents from nearby Shelby applied to be the county seat, but by popular vote it remained in Hart. Repeatedly, Shelby pursued the goal of becoming county seat in 1901, and again in 1930—but to no avail. The two towns are still in stiff competition but share the fame of Asparagus Capital by alternating years of hosting the annual National Asparagus Festival, each year trying to out do one another.

Over the years, Oceana County has held several unique claims. In 1876, pigeons came in great numbers, giving the Shelby area national notoriety as the greatest pigeon roost in the United States. For several years, this same area was noted as having the greatest potato market in northern Michigan. At one time, the county was also known as the Pea Capital of the United States. Eventually, asparagus became the main crop and in 1973, the Michigan Asparagus Advisory Board, along with local farmers, started the National Asparagus Festival to celebrate their claim of the Asparagus Capital of the World.

The festival is held every year during the second weekend in June. Harvesting of the crops usually begins around May 10 and continues for approximately six weeks. An asparagus

Left: Asparagus is considered a delicacy by many.

Right: A proud community stands behind its name.

spear can grow up to 10 inches in one day and a mature crop can be picked about 24 times in one season! Observing the harvest process is quite impressive. As many as seven people pick the crop at one time while positioned on a tractor with three seats to either side of the driver.

At harvest time, a "Mrs. Asparagus" is voted queen of the festival and chief promoter of the vegetable. She must be married or widowed, and dedicated to making asparagus a popular food. Many recipes have been born in this community for new and various ways to enjoy asparagus (for example, asparagus-based guacamole, asparagus soups and pizza, etc.). For one year, Mrs. Asparagus tours the Midwest promoting the product, the festival, and Oceana County.

Aside from the festival, Oceana County offers a variety of recreational activities and is home to the Silver Lake State Park with 2,600 acres of rolling sand dunes, where camping, boating, and hiking are all readily accessible.

& For more information contact:

Oceana County Tourism Bureau
P.O. Box 168-TB
Hart, MI 49420
(616) 873-3982

MESICK
Mushroom Capital
Wexford County

Founded in 1874 by Howard Mesick, this obscure, crossroads town has become known as the Mushroom Capital. A more precise title would be the Morel Mushroom Capital. Mesick is believed to be the only place in the world where all five varieties of the morel can be found. Mesick is located southeast of the "little finger" of Michigan in Wexford County. Both the Manistee and Pine Rivers run through the county and, along with 9 major lakes, help provide the flatlands and rolling hills with productive soil.

This region was settled in the 1860s, and in 1869 the village of Sherman was established, the first in Wexford County. It is home to the original Wexford County Courthouse and is about one mile north of Mesick. Howard Mesick was a farmer from New York who, after several years of traveling throughout Canada and Michigan, finally settled in this area. He purchased 160 acres and platted the land in 1890. In 1901, Mesick was incorporated into a village. Mr. Mesick started a sawmill and lumbering became the main industry of the region. When the railroad made its way north plans were made to make Sherman a station. Through political connections and friends that worked for the railroad, the tracks stopped at Mesick instead, thereby turning Sherman into just another small rural town.

In the 1940s and 1950s, Mesick was known as the Gladiola Capital of Michigan until a virus killed most of the flowers. Mesick began to gain a reputation for being a great area to find the elusive morel mushroom—a wild, edible mushroom prized by gourmets. They are extremely difficult to commercially reproduce, but Michigan State University and the University of Wisconsin have successfully discovered a way

A prized specimen of the morel.

in very limited quantities.

A Mushroom Festival is held during the third weekend in May. One question frequently asked by visitors is, "Where do they grow?" Long-time residents generously tell them they are found in young poplar groves, old apple orchards, near dead elm trees, along sidewalks, behind the barn, and so on.

& For more information contact:

Mesick Area Champber of Commerce
5739 North M-37
Mesick, MI 49668
(616) 885-2679

HONOR
Coho Salmon Capital
FRANKFORT
Soaring Capital
Benzie County

Benzie County, located just below the little finger of Michigan, is the home to two capital cities, Honor and Frankfort. Geographically, it is the smallest county in the state but it hosts the third largest inland lake in Michigan, Crystal Lake, at 10,423 acres. Benzie County is the home of the village of Honor, the Coho Salmon Capital of Michigan, located on the banks of the Platte River, the birthplace of the Coho Salmon. Twelve miles southwest of Honor, at Betsie Bay, is the town of Frankfort, the Soaring Capital of Michigan.

Benzie County, organized in 1869, has a population of 13,300 that triples during the summer months. It takes 30 minutes to get from one side of the county to the other, with only one traffic light along the way. Extensive lumbering began here in 1850 and continued until 1910. In 1889, the railroad came to Benzie County to transport the lumber and the first car ferry on Lake Michigan made its home port in Betsie Bay until 1981. The area's industries thrived including commercial fishing. Commercial fishing thrived for several decades, but like lumbering, the area was overfished and the industry disappeared for a time.

In the early 1960s, the alewife, a saltwater fish, made its way into the Great Lakes from the Atlantic Ocean through the St. Lawrence Seaway. Because there was no predator for this small, silvery fish, it began to over-populate and every year a large alewife die-off littered the beaches. Some areas became uninhabitable because of the decaying carcasses and unbearable smell.

Male and female Coho Salmon, predators of the alewife, were planted during the early 1960s.

In 1964, the DNR decided to introduce the Coho Salmon, a natural predator of the alewife, to the waters of Lake Michigan, to control the alewife population. They obtained eggs from the Columbia River in Oregon which were were developed in Michigan hatcheries. In the spring of 1966, 660,000 young fish were released into two different streams that led to Lake Michigan, one of which was the Platte River. In the spring of 1967, another 1.7 million more were planted. The alewife problem began to dissipate and a fishing frenzy began. The town supervisor, Sam Eberly, saw it as a great opportunity and gave the town the title of the Michigan Coho Salmon Capital. Local businesses expanded to accommodate the number of sports fishermen coming in, practically overnight.

The first annual Coho Festival was held in October 1967. Just one week before the festival, a tragedy struck the Lake Michigan shoreline around the mouth of the Platte River. Despite official storm warnings and small craft advisories, hundreds of fishermen still braved the waters. Coast Guard helicopters flew overhead announcing extreme danger. Most of the fisherman, however, were in very small boats; some were even in canoes. Battling high winds and waves up to ten feet high, many of these boats capsized and seven men drowned. Ironically, in the days following this severe storm, fishermen still risked their lives in small boats in spite of further small craft advisories. This marked the beginning of an era referred to as Coho Fever.

The Coho Salmon thrives in this area and the Fisheries Division of the Michigan DNR selected the Platte River to be the home to a new hatchery for raising salmon. It is Michigan's largest hatchery and one of the most modern, best-equipped fish-rearing facilities in the world. Annually, this hatchery produces 7.5 million salmon that are released into several rivers throughout the state; 820,000 of these are released into the Platte River. This has greatly contributed to the tremendous success of sport fishing in the Great Lakes. The annual Coho Festival is now held in August.

The peaceful flight of the glider is an awesome experience.

On the western side of Benzie County, along the high bluffs of Lake Michigan, is the town of Frankfort, the Soaring Capital of Michigan. The breezes off the lake create a steady updraft as they hit the bluffs, making it a perfect spot for soaring in glider planes. Gliders are lightweight, engineless aircraft designed for long periods of soaring after being launched from a tow plane.

Soaring became extremely popular in Frankfort during the 1930s. A gliding school and one of the largest sailplane factories in the state were established. Frankfort hosted several national meets and acquired a reputation amongst pilots as the best soaring place in the world. Almost every weekend during that era from the moment the ice melted in the spring until late November, crowds came to watch the gliders. They were usually in the air shortly after dawn; but by darkness at least one plane would still be aloft so that fires were built on the beach to guide them in to a safe landing.

Frankfort still draws soaring pilots from all over the country to test their skills and abilities. The Northwest Soaring Club of Frankfort offers introductory rides May through October. Instruction on how to become a soaring pilot is also available.

& For more information contact:

Benzie County Chamber of Commerce
P.O. Box 204
Benzonia, MI 49616
(616) 882-5801

CEDAR
Sausage Capital
Leelanau County

In the heart of Leelanau County is the town of Cedar, the Sausage Capital of Michigan. Leelanau County is known as the "Little Finger" and covers 216,000 acres in the northwest peninsula of Lower Michigan, including 43 lakes, 58 miles of streams, and 98 miles of Lake Michigan shoreline. Cedar is located near the southern end of Lake Leelanau and is surrounded by cedar forests.

In the late 1890s, Cedar was home to a small shingle mill, and with the arrival of the Manistee and Northwestern Railroad the village began to prosper. By 1910, Cedar had four sawmills and a population of over 400 people. However, due to diminishing forests, all the mills had stopped operating by 1916 and farming became the main industry.

The community was largely of Polish descent, among which was the Pleva family from Posen, Poland. In 1919, their son Joseph started a general store in Cedar that serviced the two communities of Cedar and neighboring Isadore. In 1920, their combined population was 985. His son, Andy, began a butcher shop as part of the family store in 1946. He and his brother, Ray, ran it together in a partnership until Andy retired in 1987. They developed an excellent reputation for homemade sausages. People from all over the United States began ordering their sausages from them and continue to do so. Stopping at Pleva's has become a tradition for many vacationers as the business continues to flourish, now under Ray's sole ownership.

Ray's oldest daughter, Cindy Pleva Weber, was selected as the National Cherry Queen in 1987. She became involved with promoting the cherry industry, and one evening, she asked her father how they could help it out. Ray began experiment-

Ray Pleva proudly displays his homemade sausage.

ing with various cherry and meat combinations for his sausages. He created a cherry pecan pork sausage that became a huge success. Ray continues to experiment with other meat and cherry combinations and has developed a total of 17 different cherry-meat products. One of these, Plevalean, has made Ray famous—91% lean ground beef/ground sirlon with a natural cherry blend. It has 50% less fat than a regular hamburger, 9% more protein, and 35% fewer calories. It is currently being served throughout Michigan's public schools and has gained a national reputation with today's increasingly health-conscious consumer.

Each July, Cedar hosts a weekend-long Polka Fest featuring locally-made sausage, live music and polka dancing, a softball tournament, a parade and many other festivities. Under

Dancing and entertainment spark a good time at the Cedar Polka Fest.

the tents of the Polka Fest, the true colors of Cedar are revealed. Other interests close by are Sugarloaf Ski Resort and Golf Course, the Sleeping Bear National Lakeshore Park, and abundant river and lake activities.

& For more information contact:

Leelanau Peninsula Chamber of Commerce
P.O. Box 336,
Lake Leelanau, MI 49653
(616) 256-9895
or
Pleva's Meats
Box 42
Kasson Street, Cedar, MI 49621
(616) 228-5000

TRAVERSE CITY
Cherry Capital
Grand Traverse County

Located just south of the 45th parallel, halfway between the equator and the north pole, is Traverse City, the Cherry Capital of the World. Situated on Grand Traverse Bay, it is the hub of northwest Michigan. Grand Traverse Bay consists of 250 miles of Lake Michigan shoreline, and has played a very important role in the history of the region and the development of its industries. There are more than two million cherry trees in the Grand Traverse area which produce about 40% of the tart cherries grown in the United States.

Before the arrival of white settlers, this area was a meeting and hunting place for the Ottawa, Chippewa, and Potawatomi Indians and because of their friendly relations throughout their long association, they became known as the "Three Brothers." Grand Traverse County has eight Indian village sites, six large burial grounds, and 55 mounds that have been identified by archeologists. Little effort was made to colonize the area until 1845 when the tribes held considerable portions of land. They were then granted a government treaty that allowed them to stay for a period of five years, unless there was a demand for the land by whites.

In 1846, settlers began to arrive, which led to an exodus of local Indians to Wisconsin and Canada. Lumbering in the region quickly took hold and by 1874 there were 15 steam-powered mills and one water-powered mill. However, all the sawmills were phased out by 1915 and agriculture took the lead. At the turn-of-the-century, potatoes were a very successful crop.

Meanwhile, a Presbyterian missionary, Peter Dougherty, planted the first cherry orchard in 1852, on Old Mission Peninsula just north of Traverse City, against the advice of local farmers who had tried to grow other fruit trees in the area. To everyone's surprise, the trees flourished and soon many other residents began planting orchards as well. Cherry trees can grow almost anywhere, but to grow them commercially specific conditions need to be present. Rolling hills and sandy soil are essential for drainage and large bodies of water are required to temper the cold winters and cool the orchards in the summer. These conditions are ever-present in Grand Traverse County with the blessing of its magnificent bay.

Cherry blossoms in the springtime are truly unforgettable.

The first commercial orchard was planted in 1893, near Dougherty's original plantings. By 1900, the tart cherry industry was well under way. Cherries were being shipped to

Detroit, Chicago, Milwaukee, then eventually across the country in refrigerated railroad cars. Soon, Traverse City had its own canning company for processing cherries and the shipment of fresh cherries practically came to a halt. In 1922, the Grand Traverse Packing Company introduced the first frozen cherries.

Although this region was an optimum growing region, the winters were still harsh and farmers faced winter kill, spring frost, and pests. In 1923, all of the churches in the area were asked to pray for the success of the harvest. Thus, the Blessing of the Blossoms originated one Sunday in May while the blossoms were in their peak. Today, this ceremony is still held

Bright red cherries add brilliant color to the countryside.

annually.

In 1926, a semi-formal celebration took place in honor of a rich harvest. The celebration lasted one day and consisted of a parade and the coronation of a queen. About 3,000 people attended and by 1928, the state legislature designated it the National Cherry Festival, to be held each year for a week in the beginning of July. This festival has become a way to entertain the rapidly-growing tourism industry, not to mention an increasing number of summer residents. From Interlochen

International Music Camp, to the recent restoration of the 1880s Traverse City Opera House, culture continues to flourish in Traverse City. Visitors come to the region year-round; it is a vacation playground, offering every kind of sport. The Grand Traverse area has hundreds of inland lakes, abundant recreational parks and campgrounds, and has become a mecca for vacationers from all around the world.

& For more information contact:

Traverse City Area Chamber of Commerce
202 E. Grandview Parkway
PO Box 387
Traverse City, MI 49685-0387
(616) 947-5075

LAKE CITY
Christmas Tree Capital
Missaukee County

Just southeast of Grand Traverse County, in the north central portion of the Lower Peninsula is Lake City, the Christmas Tree Capital of the Nation. Lake City is the county seat of Missaukee County and is situated along the shores of the 2,000-acre Lake Missaukee. This county is a four-season recreational area surrounded by forests, wildlife, lakes, streams, numerous parks, and campgrounds.

There are no records of permanent Indian inhabitants in the Lake City area. It was originally surveyed in 1840, but the first settlers did not arrive until the 1860s. Dairy farming and logging were the occupations of most of the early settlers. In the mills, lumber was cut into boards, broom handles, shingles, and bowls. By 1920, most of the mills had closed down and logging towns throughout the county literally disappeared overnight. The exceptionally sandy soil was not suitable for farming or livestock, but a new industry of tourism took hold, especially after World War II. Workers brought their families north by automobile for vacations and many built small cottages along the lakes. Eventually, many of these cottages were turned into year-round homes for their retirement. Hunters have discovered this region as well and return year after year.

In the 1960s and 1970s, it was found that many varieties of Christmas trees thrived in the sandy soil and local families started plantations. Sixty-two Christmas tree farms, consisting of a total of 8,000 acres, exist in Missaukee County today.

In 1984, grower Stephen VanderWeide of the Dutchman Tree Farm, just outside of Lake City, presented a 20-foot-tall spruce Christmas tree to President Ronald Reagan from his farm. He was selected after winning first a state competition, then a national competition, for the spruce category. VanderWeide and his family flew east to make the presentation of the tree along with a 4 by 8-foot scroll of white felt signed by 1,200 students in the Lake City area schools.

Christmas trees are abundant throughout northern Michigan.

In 1962, a Festival of the Pines was started in honor of Albert J. Engel and other growers and loggers in the area. Engel was a congressman from Lake City who served eight terms beginning in 1935. He was known as the "watchdog" of military spending. During World War II, he made a one-man tour of all the military bases in search of waste and extravagance. In retirement, Engel operated his own 1,400 Christmas tree plantation. He also worked hard to promote Missaukee County as the forerunner in the nation of the production of Christmas trees.

The Festival of the Pines is held each year during the third weekend of September. Contests of lumberjack skills take place including chainsaw cutting and axe throwing. There is a horseshoe competition, chili cook-off, arts and craft show, music, and dancing.

& For more information contact:

Lake City Area Chamber of Commerce
229 South Main Street
P.O. Box 52
Lake City, MI 49651-0052
(616) 839-4969

Kirtland Warbler Capital
Crawford County
Oscoda County
Roscommon County
Ogemaw County

These four counties, located in the upper middle portion of Lower Michigan, are the Kirtland Warbler Capital of the World. The Kirtland Warbler is a tiny, half-ounce yellow-breasted songbird. The heaviest concentration (90%) of this endangered bird is located in Crawford, Oscoda, Roscommon, and Ogemaw Counties until they depart for Bermuda for the winter months. These four counties are unique because they have hundreds of acres of jack pine forests and because of the partnerships that have been formed to save Michigan's rarest songbird.

The Kirtland Warbler was first spotted in this area by two trout fishermen in 1903 along the shores of the AuSable River. The bird had originally been named after the Ohio naturalist, Dr. Jarrod Kirtland, who collected a specimen on his farm in 1851. Kirtland's Warbler is noted for its harmonious, powerful, and continuous song that can be heard from a quarter-mile away. They sing three to four songs a minute from dawn until dusk, even while they are eating!

No other songbird in the world has received such official interest and controversy. Fortunately, all of this attention has resulted in a steady incline in population of these precious warblers. Environmentalists and members of the timber industry (two groups that are typically very unfriendly with one another) are working with government regulators and biologists to stabilize an environment in which the Kirtland Warbler can thrive.

Lightning causes most of the fires that occur naturally. During the great lumbering era, the branches of the felled trees were burned and the resulting fires would quickly get out of control; the only thing that stopped them were the shores of the Great Lakes. Hundreds of lives were lost, as well as homes and businesses. Periodic drought conditions, coupled by fierce winds, have also played a part in the regular devastation. However, the fires were a blessing for the jack pines, whose seeds burst from their pine cones in the intense heart of the fires creating new growth.

Jack Pines can be identified by their double 1½ needles.

In 1944, Smokey the Bear was introduced across the nation to educate the public about the prevention of forest fires following a serious forest fire in the Los Padres National Forest in Southern California. A poster was produced each year of Smokey and his message on how to prevent fires. He appeared in the Macy's Thanksgiving Day and Santa Claus Parade in New York City where, at 59 feet tall, he was viewed by over 40 million Americans on television. Smokey the Bear toys were made and a Junior Forest Ranger program was formed. He was so popular that forest fires were actually greatly reduced. With much fewer fires, trees were growing exceptionally tall.

Strangely enough, the Kirtland Warbler is dependent upon fire because it hides its nest in the undergrowth of the lower branches of young jack pines amongst huckleberry bushes and sweet grass. Typically they stay close to their nesting habitat until they migrate south for the winter. Thus the reduction of forest fires altered the Kirtland's Warbler habitat and the population took a significant plunge as a result.

Kirtland's Warbler

Another cause for the near extinction of the songbird is the nesting patterns of the Brown-headed Cowbird. The female Cowbird lays her eggs in other birds' nests, often removing eggs that are already in the nest before depositing her own. The Cowbird's eggs are then hatched and fed by the host bird. Some birds are able to identify the impostor eggs and reject them, but the Kirtland Warblers lack this capability and are not able to raise their own young under these circumstances. In 1972, Cowbirds began to be trapped in order to control this situation. Before trapping, 70% of the warbler's nests were occupied by Cowbird eggs; the occupant rate is now at 6%.

More importantly, however, the restoration of the Kirtland Warbler habitat has begun. State and federal agencies set controlled fires and privately-owned logging companies cut the timber to simulate the effects of forest fires. Several million jack pines have been planted to provide a nesting site for the warbler. An annual census is conducted by the U.S. Forest Service and the Fish & Wildlife Service, along with a group of volunteers, during the first two weeks in June. It looks as though all of these efforts are paying off. The 1974 census reported 167 males but in 1993, 485 males were counted, an increase of 220%. The Kirtland Warbler will remain on the endangered species list until there are 1,000 pairs of males and females.

A festival is held during the third weekend in May to honor the little bird. It is organized by Kirtland Community College in Roscommon and several events, free of charge, are offered such as bird watching, nature tours, wildlife and environmental workshops, and a Kirtland's Warbler maze. A festival raffle is held and the winner receives an all expense paid trip for two to the birds' winter home, the Bahamas. The best time to view the Kirtland Warbler is from May 20 to June 20. A self-guided, 48-mile viewing tour through the jack pine ecosystem near Mio offers great potential for spotting the warbler, and many other birds as well, including the bald eagle. Guided tours are also available.

& For more information contact:

Fish & Wildlife Service (517) 351-2555
Forest Service (517) 826-3252
or
Kirtland Community College
10775 N. Saint Helen Road
Roscommon, MI 48563
(517) 275-5121

Cross-Country Ski Capital Iosco County

Iosco County is the Cross-Country Ski Capital of Michigan. It is located along the shores of Lake Huron just above Bay City and the thumb region. The famous AuSable River flows through the county and meets Lake Huron at the town of Oscoda, the end point of the AuSable International Canoe Marathon. Iosco County was designated as the Cross-Country Ski Capital by the state legislature in the mid-1980s because it possesses the longest network of groomed trails in the state. The county is a year-round recreational paradise for many other sports as well.

Robert La Salle was the first to explore this area in 1679, and his ship, the *Griffon,* was the first sailing vessel on the Great Lakes. The first white settlers were French fur traders who arrived here as early as 1800. An American Fur Company outpost was located at the mouth of the AuSable. The Chippewa Indians deeded the land to the United States government in the Saginaw Treaty of 1819. The county was surveyed in 1840 and named Iosco, which means "water of light," in 1843.

Life was exceptionally solitary for the early pioneers. In 1860, there were 175 people living in Iosco County. However, as travel to the region became easier by boat, stage coach and train, post offices, schoolhouses and churches were built along the shoreline. The end of the Civil War brought many new frontiersmen. Lumber mills, fisheries and eventually, salt and gypsum mining, along with plenty of manpower, brought new and sudden growth. In 1890, the county had a population of 15,224!

Tourism had never occurred to the residents as a source of revenue. But, at the turn-of-the-century, three families who were affiliated with the Detroit and Mackinac Railroad devel-

Cross-country skiers enjoy Michigan's many trails throughout the northern region.

oped the Beach Club, located in what is now East Tawas. Summer excursions on the bay became an attraction. Tourists arrived with basket dinners to spend the day at the beach. Soon it became known as a recreation area for hunting, fishing, boating and eventually, cross-country skiing.

Iosco County offers 100 miles of groomed cross-country ski trails. Two of the most significant trails are the Corsair Trail complex and Eagle Run. The Corsair Trails, 26 miles long, consist of gentle rolling hills that pass through an abundance of wildlife. An early pioner settlement was located in this system and the Silver Valley Trail goes by a pioneer graveyard. Tawas, the closest community, is seven miles southeast of Corsair.

The Eagle Run trail system is a loop that runs through a very remote area and has scenic views of the AuSable River. There are trails for both beginners and intermediate skiers. The town of Oscoda is just three miles east of Eagle Run. For snowmobilers there are well-marked trails in Iosco County that interconnect with over 1,000 miles of trails throughout northern Michigan. During the snow-free seasons, the trails are perfect for hiking, camping and fishing.

& For trail conditions, call (800) 55-Tawas.

& For other information call:

Huron Shores Ranger Station
(517) 739-0728
or
Visitor Information Center
4440 North U.S. 23
Oscoda, MI 48750
(800) 235-GOAL

GRAYLING
Canoe Capital
Crawford County

In the very center of northern Lower Michigan lies the town of Grayling, the Canoe Capital of the World, and one of the state's leading recreational areas. The waters of the AuSable River are the source of its capital claim. Starting from Grayling, this sparkling river flows 120 windy miles east to the town of Oscoda and to the shores of Lake Huron.

The Chippewa and Ottawa Indians made this area their home, calling the AuSable "Mud-au-bee-be-ton-ange" which means "coming from the interior to the lake." The early pioneers traded with the Indians and found them extremely friendly and helpful, especially during the severe winters.

It did not take long for word to get out that the AuSable, with its access to Lake Huron, was ideal for carrying logs. The land provided some of the finest timber found throughout the Great Lakes region and the supply seemed limitless. The town of Grayling was established, named after a fish that once frequented the AuSable. From 1867 to 1883, 1.3 billion feet of logs were floated down the AuSable, an average of 83 million feet per year! Sidewalks, houses, and boxcars were made of wood during this era. In 1882, more than 74% of the tonnage on railroad cars were products of the forests. The peak year for the mills in Grayling was 1890. But by the turn-of-the-century, it had all ended due to the depletion of the great forests. In 1910, there was one final log drive down the AuSable of sunken timber that had been reclaimed from the river's bottom.

Logging towns disappeared virtually overnight, but Grayling made a great effort to stay alive and to attract newcomers. The Detroit, the Lansing, and the Northern railroads advertised and Grayling became known as a perfect place for family vacations and hunting. Even though the soil was very poor, the railroads promoted property as great farmland at inexpensive prices and raved about the good citizens of Grayling. It was also rumored that there was oil in Crawford County. Incidentally, it was eventually discovered in the 1940s in Beaver Creek Township near the Upper AuSable.

Civil War Veterans were offered land grants near Grayling and soon times were changing. Unfortunately, the environment began to reflect the signs of these times. With the diminishing forests statewide, many species of wildlife lost their natural habitat. Deer were decimated by both wolves and ambitious hunters.

The loggers, however, were solely responsible for the loss of the game fish, the Grayling. The Grayling is a tender-mouthed fish with pure white meat. The brilliantly-colored fish is still found in these waters but in such small numbers that it is illegal to catch them. Many years ago the Grayling was considered one of the north's most prized game fish. However, when the great pines along the river were felled, significant erosion occurred and the Grayling could not withstand the mud and increased temperature of the no-longer-shaded water. Further, when the logs came down the river, the Grayling's spawning beds were raked and its eggs destroyed. The characteristics of the AuSable had been changed so drastically that when the state first tried to replant them, the fish did not survive. Eventually, a second growth of timber helped tremendously.

Grayling has another claim to sports fame as well. A sportsman named Fred Bear visited the area. He had new ideas for designing hunting bows and arrows. He started a factory there on a five-acre site, eventually employing 200 employees, and for a time Grayling became the Archery Capital of the Nation.

In September 1947, a canoe race departing from Grayling and finishing in Oscoda via the AuSable, was started. At that time, some of the townspeople were extremely skeptical—they thought that it was very unlikely to be a success. Much to their surprise, 46 teams participated in the first Weyerhauser

Enthusiastic canoeists are negotiating their next obstacle.

AuSable River Marathon and the winners (both from Grayling) finished after paddling for 21 hours and 3 minutes! For 50 years, the race has continued to attract over 50 teams and nearly 30,000 fans annually. This 120-mile nonstop marathon begins at 9:00 p.m. on Saturday evening during the last weekend of July. The race is held at night to avoid the hot summer heat and the humidity of the day. Competitors paddle an estimated 55,000 strokes for 14 hours. It all begins in downtown Grayling with a two-block running start to the river, where the teams throw their canoes into the water and paddle ferociously to get a head start.

Meanwhile, the fans scream and cheer the canoeists on all night long throughout what is often referred to as the "world's toughest spectator race." There are several viewing spots along the AuSable, including bridges and portage points at the river's six hydroelectric power plant dams. The most exciting vantage point is, of course, the finish line along the riverbanks in Oscoda. Prior to the finish of what is known as North America's longest, toughest, nonstop canoe race, a pancake breakfast is served for the spectators. The festivities do not end following the conclusion of the marathon. An amateur canoe competition is held, as well as events for young children, a flea market, and an array of refreshments.

The international marathon is the main event but the entire month of July is called Canoe Marathon Month during which there are several other races held for all ages and levels of canoeists and for one- and two-person divisions. Canoes and paddles are produced in Grayling and are for sale or for rent on both the AuSable and Manistee Rivers.

Area craftsman enjoy the art of building canoes.

For wintertime fun, Grayling is host to the longest toboggan run in Michigan. This 3,000 foot run sweeps tobogganists up to speeds of 100 miles per hour! Another notable attraction of Crawford County is the Hartwick Pines State Park, one of Michigan's six natural wonders. Here, 85 acres of the virgin white pines that once covered the state, remain standing proud and very tall. The park displays a reconstructed lumber camp with a collection of logging equipment dating back to the 1870s. A preserved logging wheel that won awards at the Chicago World's Fair in 1893 and many other relics, such as sleighs for moving logs in the winter, can be found there as well.

& For more information call:

Grayling Area Visitors Council
(800) 937-8837

& For information on canoe races contact:

A.R.I.C.M.
P.O. Box 911
Grayling, MI 49738
(517) 348-4425

ROGERS CITY
Chinook Salmon Capital
POSEN
Potato Capital
ONAWAY
Sturgeon Capital
Presque Isle County

Southeast of the Mackinac Bridge in the northern Lower Peninsula is one of Michigan's most unique and undiscovered counties, Presque Isle. Encompassing 560 square acres of lakes, streams, rivers, and forests, Presque Isle has the distinction of being the only county in Michigan to represent three capital cities: Rogers City, Posen, and Onaway. Rogers City, the Chinook Salmon Capital, is located along the shores of Lake Huron. Sixteen miles south of Rogers City is Posen, the Potato Capital. The last, but far from least, just 20 miles west of Rogers City, is Onaway, the Sturgeon Capital. The entire region is a true sportsman's paradise.

Presque Isle County's early history is typical of the rest of the state. Agriculture, limestone mining, hunting, and fishing became the leading industries. Today, they still play as important role as they did 75 years ago. The limestone quarry is the largest in the world.

Rogers City, the county seat, is the Chinook Salmon (also known as the King Salmon) Capital of Michigan. The Chinook Salmon is one of the several "sportfish" that were introduced to the Great Lakes by the Department of Natural Resources in the early 1960s. Similar to the Coho Salmon, the Chinook is native to the waters of the Pacific Northwest. It is sought after not only for its size and fighting capability but for its unique flavor and taste as well. The main physical differences between the two fish are that the Chinook has black gums and the Coho has white, and the Chinook has black spots over its entire tail while the Coho has black spots on the upper portion of its tail. Otherwise, they are very similar and are often confused. Every August, Rogers City hosts an annual Salmon Fishing Tournament and anglers from all over the Midwest participate.

A short drive south of the county seat is Posen, the Potato Capital of Michigan. One of several northern Michigan Polish settlements, it was established in 1870. Potato farming

Michigan potatoes are always a favorite at every meal.

became the mainstay and by the late 1930s, Posen became known as the Potato Capital. Many different varieties of potatoes are grown here, the most important being the "Onaway." It is a round, white potato that is very hardy and is good for long storage (it can last from September to March). In addition, the region also grows Idahos, Reds, Burbanks, Russetts, and Yukon Golds. Approximately 1,000 semi-truck loads are shipped out of Posen each year, the equivalent of 45 million tons! A Potato Festival is held during the weekend after Labor Day, a tradition that has prevailed for 47 years and which attracts tens of thousands of people each year.

West of Rogers City, via State Route 68, and just south of Black Lake, is Onaway, the Sturgeon Capital of Michigan. The Lake Sturgeon (also known as the Rock or Red Sturgeon) lives in lakes and streams from the Mississippi River to the Great Lakes and eastward to the St. Lawrence River. The fish is olive-brown with a reddish tinge and a white stomach. Along its back and sides are horny scutes, or shields, that are light or white in color. The average sturgeon is about 3.5 feet long and weighs 50-60 pounds. The state record weighed in at 193 pounds. A sturgeon matures at approximately 20 years and can live as long as 150 years.

During the 19th century, these fish were speared in the springtime during their ascent up the rivers for spawning. In the early part of the 20th century, sturgeon were ruthlessly harvested to meet the demands of the caviar market and the Sturgeon nearly became extinct. The Department of Natural Resources imposed strict restrictions: one Sturgeon per person per season which is the entire month of February. Also, because many inland lakes were closed off due to the construction of dams, the Sturgeon has become trapped in small lakes such as Burt, Mullet, and Black Lakes which are located in Presque Isle County.

Diehard sports fishermen flock to this region year after year to spear the elusive fish through the ice. Sometimes, it is several years before they even have their first encounter with a Sturgeon. Just catching a glimpse of one is often enough to entice them back again and again. The average number of Sturgeon caught in a good year on Black Lake is 16 or 17. During the last weekend of February, the Annual Sturgeon Shivaree is held at Onaway State Park to celebrate the revival of the great fish and those who seek them with great dedication.

& For more information contact:

Onaway Area Chamber of Commerce
State Street
Onaway, MI 49765
or
Rogers City Traveler's and Visitor's Bureau
540 W. 3rd
Rogers City, MI 49779
(517) 734-2535
(800) 622-4148 (in Michigan)

UPPER PENINSULA

Bald Eagle Capital
Fungus Capital
Iron County

Iron County has two capital claims: the Bald Eagle Capital of the Midwest and the Fungus Capital of the World. The county is located in the western portion of the Upper Peninsula, bordering Wisconsin at its southwestern edge. Totaling approximately 750,000 acres (excluding surface water), the county consists of hilly terrain formed by glacial deposits and is covered by forest and farmland.

In 1885, Iron County was named after its most valuable resource—iron ore. Mining was the main industry until the last ore shipment in November 1979. The town of Iron River was designated as the temporary county seat which angered residents in nearby Crystal Falls. The rivalry that grew between the two communities led to the theft of the county records by a group of Crystal Falls citizens (including the sheriff and township supervisor) on a cold winter night in 1887. The dispute was finally resolved by a general election in the spring of 1889. Crystal Falls was designated as the new county seat by a mere five vote margin. To this day, the rivalry continues between the two cities.

One hundred years later, in 1985, Iron County was named the Bald Eagle Capital of the Midwest. In 1988, 20 active nests were found with 22 young eaglets. The population continues to grow and just recently the great bird has been taken off the endangered species list. With 528 small lakes and numerous streams teeming with fish, Iron County is a perfect breeding ground for the eagle. Although specific locations for nesting cannot be given, the eagle can be seen soaring above the many lakes and streams throughout this magnificent county.

A good example of the American Bald Eagle's habitat in the upper Great Lakes region.

In the southeastern portion of Iron County is the "Humungus Fungus." The fungus was discovered in 1988 by Myron L. Smith and James B. Anderson while doing research for the U.S. Navy. It was identified as *armillaria bulbosa*, one of about ten *armillaria* species in North America. This discovery thus gave another claim to Iron County, the Fungus Capital of the World. The fungus is over 30 acres in size, weighs nearly 100 tons, and is entirely underground! It is believed to be the largest and oldest living thing in the world, very possibly growing since the end of the last Ice Age. In the fall, the fungus produces the edible "honey mushroom." Each year, at the end of September, the "Humungus Fungus Festival" is held in Crystal Falls to celebrate the arrival of the mushroom. The weekend's festivities includes the Heavy Weight Horse Pull, the Mushroom Cook-off, live entertainment, and many other events.

Iron County is an all-season recreational area offering something for everyone. The city of Caspian is host to the

Upper Peninsula's largest outdoor museum—a pioneer village, featuring the Lee Leblanc Wildlife Art Gallery. Rich in natural beauty, Iron County is home to six major waterfalls. A circle tour for viewing the falls has been developed by Dan

Waterfalls can be discovered throughout the Upper Peninsula.

Robbins of the Iron County Chamber of Commerce. Fishing, hunting, hiking, camping, snowmobiling, and skiing are all available in this Upper Peninsula paradise.

& For more information contact:

Crystal Falls Business Association
c/o Melson's Copy Center
1353 West U.S. 2
Crystal Falls, MI 49920 (906) 875-4405
or
Iron County Chamber of Commerce
50 E. Genesee Street
Iron River, MI 49935
(800) 255-3620

Deer Capital
Dairy Capital
Menominee County

Menominee County is both the Deer Capital of Michigan and the Dairy Capital of the Upper Pennisula. It is the southernmost county of the Upper Peninsula, and consists mostly of flat terrain mixed with wetlands and woods. It borders Lake Michigan to the east and Wisconsin to the west.

The county seat is also named Menominee. It received its name, which means "wild rice," from one of the Indian tribes that occupied the banks of the Menominee River (the earliest settlements date back to over 3,000 years). In 1796, an Indian trader/agent of a fur company set up a trading post on the other side of the river in what is now Marinette, Wisconsin. Later the post was moved to the Michigan side.

In 1856, the area's timber was ruthlessly cut, milled and shipped, mostly by big companies from the East. For a time, Menominee became known as the White Pine Capital of the World. By 1930, the last of the sawmills had closed but new industries followed. Dairies sprouted up all over the county and in the 1970s, Menominee became known as the Dairy Capital of the World. That title has also faded now as many of the smaller dairies have been bought out by larger dairies of Wisconsin. Presently, the county still holds claim to the Dairy Capital of the Upper Peninsula, with approximately 180 dairies in operation.

A large number of these dairies are located near the village of Stephenson, a quaint country town with many friendly

Dairy farming is a lucrative industry in the Upper Peninsula.

faces. The community has thrived throughout the years, beginning with logging and then dairy farming. In 1933, Stephenson was the smallest village in the world that owned its own municipalities, which was quite impressive at that time.

The Michigan Department of Natural Resources has a field office in Stephenson. As a wildlife technician explained, although Menominee is the Deer Capital of Michigan, "it is nothing to celebrate." The deer population is the densest per acre than any other county in Michigan. There are numerous car/

Three hunters proudly display their prizes.

deer accidents (over 1000 in 1994), especially in the early morning and evening hours. The flip side is that it is a deer hunter's paradise and each year thousands of hunters flock to this area, bringing much needed revenue. Even with the many "trophies" that these hunters bring home, the deer population continues to multiply.

Fishing is also a popular sport. The Menominee River and Lake Michigan offer a variety of many species of fish: Sturgeon, Northern Pike, Walleye, Bass, Brook Trout, Brown Trout, and Rainbow Trout.

& For more information contact:

Menominee Area Chamber of Commerce
1005 Tenth Avenue
Menominee, Michigan 49858
(906) 863-2679

AFTERWORD

We realize that we may not have included all of the capital cities that are in the state. Several were brought to our attention after it was too late to include them in this book. They include:

Algonac, Pickerel Capital
Atlanta, Elk Capital
Fairview, Turkey Capital
Tecumseh, Refrigeration Capital

Wild turkeys stop traffic in northern Michigan.

These capital cities will be included in our next book. If you think your city or region deserves to be included as well, please let us know:

Melissa Stimon
Box 494
Leland, MI 49654

M. F. Chatfield
Box 88
Leland, MI 49654

ACKNOWLEDGEMENTS

The information and help these people and organizations provided were greatly appreciated by the authors. All area Chambers of Commerce and Visitor's Bureaus were extremely valuable resources as well.

Algonac-Clay Historical Society; John P. Amrhein; Andy's Antiques, Allen, Michigan; Amber R. Bailey; Lena Ball; Les Barnes; Frank Bayee; Wayne and Shirley Beachum; Greg Bordener; Cece Chatfield; Chet & Patty Chetcuti; Virginia Christianson; Wanda Edie; Johnny Eggert; Dorothy Everett; Alice M. Fewins; Robert George; Bob and Martha Graham; Diana Green; Joy Hamilton; Jean A. Harvey-Clark; Kay Haven; Lynette Kelley; Tom & Carol Kolarik; Dave Kleweno; Dale Kuenzli; Catherine A. Larson; John A. McGill; Marvel Money; Terry Money; Art and Lee Niffenegger; Earl Norling; Chuck O'Connor; Gordon Olson; Platte River State Fish Hatchery; Ray Pleva; Virgie Purchase; Dan Robbins; Joan Rutherford; Pete Sandman; Richard Schinkel; Sherry Sponseller; Deanna Stoll; Bethany Styer; Skip & Lynn Telegard; Barb Thoms; Albert Voras; Kathy Walicki; Jack R.Westbrook; Tim William; Karen Williams; Diane R. Wykes; Bruce Wymer; and Greg Yost.

NOTES

NOTES

NOTES

NOTES